IN DISGUISE

HISTORY'S FAMOUS FEMALE SPIES

By

VARIOUS

Read & Co.

This edition is published by Read & Co. History,
an imprint of Read & Co.

British Library Cataloguing-in-Publication Data
A catalogue record for this book is available
from the British Library.

Read & Co. is part of Read Books Ltd.
For more information visit
www.readandcobooks.co.uk

CONTENTS

BELLE BOYD

THE CONFEDERATE GIRL WHO SAVED STONEWALL JACKSON

THAT brilliant writer, Gilbert Chesterton, in one of his paradoxical essays said that a fact, if looked at fiercely, may become an adventure. It is certain that the most important facts in the life of Belle Boyd, the Confederate spy, constitute some of the most thrilling adventures in the great conflict between the sections—the Civil War in the United States.

She was only a girl when the flag was fired on at Sumter and her father and all the members of her family immediately enlisted in the Confederate army. When the Union troops took possession of Martinsburg, Belle Boyd found herself unwillingly inside the Federal lines. She had no formal commission from any of the Southern officers, but circumstances and her ardent nature made her an intense partisan of what was to be "The Lost Cause."

During the occupation of Martinsburg, she shot a Union soldier, who, she claimed, had insulted a Southern woman. From that moment until the close of the war she was actively engaged either as a spy, a scout or an emissary of the Confederacy. On more than one occasion she attracted the attention of Secretary of War Stanton, and although she served a term in a military prison, she seems to have been treated with unusual leniency. After the war she escaped to England, where she published her autobiography, bitterly assailing the victorious North.

It was in Martinsburg that Belle Boyd first began her work for the Confederacy. The Union officers sometimes left their swords and pistols about the houses which they occupied, and later were surprised and mystified at the strange disappearance of the weapons. They little thought that this mere slip of a girl was the culprit. Still later they were amazed to find that these same swords and pistols had found their way into the hands of the enemy and were being used against them.

But aside from this Belle Boyd made it her business to pick up all the information that was possible concerning the movements and the plans of the Union forces. Every scrap of news she obtained was promptly conveyed to General J. E. B. Stuart and other Confederate officers.

It was about the time of the battle of Bull Run that the Confederate general in command fixed upon Front Royal as a site for a military hospital. Belle Boyd was one of the nurses and many a fevered brow felt the touch of her cool hand and more than one stricken soldier afterwards testified to the loving care he received from this remarkable woman.

Later, Front Royal became the prize of the Union army, and Belle Boyd naturally fell under suspicion. Some remarks of her activities had already reached the front, and the officers kept her under close scrutiny. Fortunately, as she thought, she had been provided with a pass which would permit her to leave the place. Accordingly, the second day after the arrival of the Unionists she packed her grip and prepared to leave the town. As she came from the house she was halted by a Union officer named Captain Bannon.

"Is this Miss Belle Boyd?"

"Yes."

"Well, I am the Assistant Provost Marshal, and I regret to say that orders have been issued for your detention. It is my duty to inform you that you cannot proceed until your case has been investigated."

This did not suit the young woman at all. She opened her pocketbook and produced a bit of pasteboard.

"I have here a pass from General Shields. Surely that should be sufficient to permit me to leave the city."

The young officer was perplexed. He did not care to repudiate a pass issued by General Shields, and at the same time did not wish to disobey the instructions which he had received from his immediate chief.

"I hardly know what to do," he said. "However, I am going to Baltimore with a squad of men in the morning. I will take you with me and when we get there turn you over to General Dix."

This program was carried out and the Confederate spy was given a free trip to the monumental city, which she did not want. She was compelled to remain in Baltimore for some time, being kept constantly under the closest supervision. Finally, however, General Dix gave her permission to return to her home. There was no direct evidence against her and it was considered a waste of time and energy to keep her under guard. She was escorted to the boundaries of her old home by two Union soldiers. It was twilight when she arrived at the Shenandoah River. The effects of the war were to be seen on every side. The bridges had been destroyed, and they only managed to cross the river by means of a temporary ferry boat that had been pressed into service.

When she reached her home she found that it had been appropriated as a headquarters by General Shields and the members of his staff. He treated her courteously and said that no harm would befall her if she was discreet and attended to her own business. She was told that a small house adjoining the family dwelling had been set aside for her use, and that the soldiers would be given orders not to molest her in any way.

But the young daughter of the Confederacy kept her eyes and ears open and the night before the departure of General Shields, who was to give battle to General Jackson, she learned that a council of war was to be held in the drawing-room of the Boyd home. Just over this apartment was a bedroom containing a large closet. On the night of the council she managed to make her way to this room and slipped into the closet. A hole had been bored through the floor, whether by design or otherwise she was unable to tell. However, she immediately determined to take advantage of what she considered a providential situation.

When the council assembled the girl got down on her hands and knees in the bottom of the closet and placed her ear near the hole in the floor. To her great satisfaction she found that she could distinctly hear all of the conversation. The conference between the Union officers lasted for hours, but she remained motionless and silent until it had been concluded. When the scraping movement of the chairs on the floor below was heard she knew that everything was over so came out of her place of concealment. She was tired and her limbs were so stiff from remaining in that cramped position so long that it was all she could do to move. But she was full of grit and determination and as soon as the coast was clear she hurried across the courtyard and made the best of her way to her own room in the little house and wrote down in cipher—a cipher of her own—everything of importance that she had overheard.

After that it was but a matter of a few minutes to decide on her course of action. She knew that it would be extremely dangerous to call a servant or to do anything that might arouse the officers, who had by this time gone to bed, so she went to the stables and saddled a horse herself, and galloped away in the direction of the mountains. The moon was shining when she started on this wild ride. She had in her possession passes which she had obtained from time to time for Confederate soldiers who were returning south. Without them it would have been impossible for her to have accomplished her purpose. Before she had gone a half mile she was halted by a Federal sentry. He grabbed the bridle of her horse and cried out:

"Where are you going?"

"I am going to visit a sick friend," was the ready response.

"You can't do it," he cried. "You ought to know that you can't leave this place without a pass."

"But I have one," she said, with an engaging smile, and drew out the piece of pasteboard.

The guard looked at it dubiously, but it was in proper form and contained the necessary signature and he grudgingly permitted her to continue on her journey.

Twice again she was halted by sentinels and each time she told the same story and underwent the same experience. Once clear of the chain of sentries she whipped her horse and hurried ahead for a distance of fifteen miles. At that time the animal was in a perfect lather and when she pulled up in front of the frame house which was the dwelling place of her friends the horse was panting and trembling from the unusual exertion. She leaped from the animal's back and going to the door rapped on it with the butt end of her riding whip. There was no reply, so she hammered harder than ever. Presently a window in the second story was cautiously opened and a head poked out and a voice called:

"Who's there?"

"Belle Boyd, and I have important intelligence to give to Colonel Ashby."

"My dear Belle!" shrieked the voice from the window. "Where in the world did you come from and how did you get here?"

"Oh, I forced the sentries," was the reply, in a matter of fact voice.

Within sixty seconds the girl was in the house and receiving refreshments and telling her strange story to her wondering friend. The horse in the meantime was taken to the stable by a negro and carefully groomed and fed. Only after these important details had been attended to was the girl permitted to tell her story.

"I must see Colonel Ashby," she said in conclusion, "and if you can tell me where to find him I will go at once."

She was informed that the Confederate officer and his party were in the woods about a half mile distant from the place in which they were sitting. Just as the girl was ready to go the front door was thrown open and Colonel Ashby stood before her.

He looked at her as if she were a ghost and then finally burst forth in amazement:

"My God, Miss Belle, is that you? Where did you come from? Did you drop from the clouds?"

"No," she said smilingly, "I didn't. I came on horseback and I have some very important information."

Whereupon she related the details of the council that had taken place in the Boyd home, and then told the story of her mad ride through the night. She concluded by handing him the cipher, which he said would be communicated to his superior officers at once.

After that she insisted on mounting her horse and returning home again. It was more than two hours' ride, during which time she ran the blockade of the sleeping sentries with comparative success. Just at dawn when she was in sight of her home one of the sentries she was passing called out:

"Halt or I'll shoot!"

But she did not halt. On the contrary she whipped her horse until it fairly leaped through the air. She felt that the man was leveling his gun in her direction. She lay flat on her horse's back with her arms around his neck, and this was done in the very nick of time, for at that same moment a hot bullet came singing past her ears. That was the only serious interruption. In a few minutes she had reached the grounds surrounding the Boyd home. Fortunately no one was in sight. She hurried into the house and went to bed in her aunt's room just at the break of dawn.

Two days later General Shields marched south with the idea of laying a trap to catch General Jackson. Once again the fearless girl determined to carry the information she possessed to her Confederate friends. Major Tyndale, at that time Provost Marshal, gave Belle Boyd and her cousin a pass to Winchester. Once there a gentleman of standing in the community called on her and handing her a package, said:

"Miss Belle, I am going to ask you to take these letters, and send them through the lines to the Confederate army. One of them is of supreme importance and I beseech you to try and get it safely to General Jackson."

After the exercise of considerable ingenuity she managed to get a pass to Front Royal. To add to the romantic feature of the business a young Union officer, who admired the girl, offered to escort her to her destination. They went in a carriage, but before starting she made it a point to conceal the Jackson letter inside her dress. The other letters, which were of comparatively small importance, she handed to the Union officer with the remark that she would take them from him when they reached Front Royal. On the way, as she feared, they were stopped by a sentinel. The Union admirer of the Confederate spy explained that they had a pass which would permit them to proceed on their way, but the zealous sentinel insisted on searching them and was highly indignant when he discovered the compromising letters in the hands of the young man. He insisted upon confiscating them, but in the excitement forgot all about the girl, and she was permitted to go unmolested, carrying with her the precious letter intended for General Jackson.

Afterwards she laughingly expressed contrition for having involved an ardent admirer in such a serious plight, but excused herself on the ground that all was fair in war as well as in love. Fortunately, the young man, who was a perfectly loyal Northern soldier, was given the credit of having discovered the papers, which were valuable to his superior officers. Thus do we sometimes make a virtue of necessity.

After Belle Boyd had been in Front Royal for several days she learned that the Confederates were coming to that place, but she also discovered that General Banks was at Strasbourg with 4,000 men; that White was at Harper's Ferry; Shields and Geary a short distance away, and Frémont below the valley. At a spot which was the vital point all of the separate divisions were expected to meet and coöperate in the destruction of General Jackson. She realized that the Confederates were in a most critical situation and that unless the officers in command were aware of the facts they might rush into a trap which meant possible annihilation.

With characteristic promptness she decided on her plan of action. She rushed out to warn the approaching Confederates. On that occasion she wore a dark blue dress with a fancy white apron over it which made her a shining mark for bullets. The Federal pickets fired at her but missed and a shell burst near her at one time, but she threw herself flat on the ground and thus escaped what seemed to be sure death. Presently she came within sight of the approaching Confederates and waved her bonnet as a signal.

Major Harry Douglass, whom she knew, galloped up and received from her the information, which he immediately transmitted to General Jackson. The result of all this was a rout of the Union forces.

It was in this battle of Bull Run which followed soon afterwards that General Bee, as he rallied his men, shouted:

"There's Jackson standing like a stonewall!"

From that time, as has been aptly said, the name he received in a baptism of fire displaced that which he had received in a baptism of water.

The number of Union men engaged in the battle of Bull Run was about 18,000, and the number of Confederates somewhat greater.

Soon after the engagement the young woman received the following letter, which she prized until the hour of her death.

> Miss Belle Boyd:
>
> I thank you for myself and for the army, for the immense service you have rendered your country to-day.
>
> Hastily, I am your friend,
> T. J. Jackson, C. S. A.

Shortly before the close of the war Belle Boyd was captured

and imprisoned. She escaped and made her way to England. In London she attracted the attention of George Augustus Sala, the famous writer. She had been married in the meantime and her husband, Lieutenant Hardage of the Confederate army, was among those taken prisoner by the Union forces.

While abroad she became financially embarrassed; indeed, at one time she was reduced to actual want. A stranger in a strange land, sick in mind and body, she was in a pitiable condition. Mr. Sala wrote a letter to the *London Times* explaining her sad state and roundly abusing the United States Government which had, he said, not only imprisoned her husband but was also "barbarous enough to place him in irons."

British sympathies were very strongly with the South at that time, and as a result of this plea provision was made for the immediate wants of the famous spy. After the war she disappeared from the public gaze, and some years later died in comparative obscurity.

A Chapter from
The World's Greatest Military Spies and Secret Service Agents, 1917
By George Barton

LYDIA DARRAH

THE BRAVE QUAKERESS WHO SAVED WASHINGTON'S ARMY FROM DESTRUCTION

WHILE the British occupied Philadelphia during the Revolutionary War most of their time was given to the pleasures of life. It was this fact that caused Franklin to observe with characteristic shrewdness that "Howe had not taken Philadelphia but Philadelphia had taken Howe." There was, however, one serious attempt made to destroy Washington's army during the period and, curiously enough, it was frustrated by the courage, the wit and the promptness of a brave Quakeress.

When the British took possession of the city the officers appropriated the most desirable dwellings for their headquarters. Thus General Harris practically confiscated the home of General Cadwallader, on Second Street, four doors below Spruce. Directly opposite this, on the corner of Little Dock Street, was the quaint home of William and Lydia Darrah, who were members of the Society of Friends, whose members, it need scarcely be said, have a profound repugnance to war.

By one of those little ironies which constantly mock our lives, the Adjutant-General of the British army decided to make his home with the Darrahs. By the polite fiction which sometimes prevails in time of war as well as of peace, both pretended to be delighted with the arrangement. It is certain that the Englishman found a desirable and well kept colonial home for his temporary habitation, while the Darrahs soon discovered that whatever else he might be, their war guest was a gentleman.

Lydia Darrah had the reputation of being a Whig, and she

gloried in it. She made no secret of her feelings to her lodger, and one day when he reproached her with her want of loyalty to the mother country, she exclaimed with spirit:

"I hope thee is beaten—thee deserve to be for coming across the ocean to subdue a liberty-loving people."

He laughed at this outburst and remarked:

"I was beginning to flatter myself that you and your husband looked upon me as a friend."

"And so we do. We detest the sin while pitying the sinner. Though we consider thee as a public enemy, we regard thee as a private friend. While we detest the cause thee fights for, we wish well to thy personal interest and safety."

"Oh!" he cried, jovially. "That sounds better. You are really a friend of the King."

"Thee must not feel flattered," she said gravely. "We are for the Colonists. Thee knows that every unnecessary expense has been retrenched in this house. Tea has not been drunk since last Christmas. Nor have I bought a new cap or gown since your defeat at Lexington. Be assured that such is the feeling of American women."

The Adjutant-General could not but admire the spirit of such a woman. Whatever else she might be she was not deceitful. She did not attempt to curry favor with the British. It rather pleased him to permit her to indulge in what might be considered treasonable sentiments. No matter how radical might be her views there could be no danger from this sweet-faced little woman with the poke bonnet and the drab dress. And, moreover, even when most spirited, there was no bitterness or vindictiveness in her tone or manner. As he gazed at her he felt that the serenity of her countenance was truly an outward sign of the tranquillity of her life.

Among other things, the Adjutant-General had arranged for a room on the first floor to be used as a sort of conference chamber for the British officers. Here groups of the leading redcoats were wont to assemble, by candle-light, for the purpose of discussing plans of campaigns. Several of these gatherings had been held without attracting any particular attention from Lydia Darrah.

Early in December, 1777, there was a strange halt in the round of pleasure among the British officers in Philadelphia. The men were drilled and organized as if in anticipation of a coming movement. The indifference and indolence of the previous months gave way to activity all along the line. Lydia, who was a true patriot, observed these signs with genuine distress. She could not but feel that it boded ill to her countrymen.

It was on the 2nd of December that the Adjutant-General sent for her. She noticed that he was serious and preoccupied.

"I wish to tell you," he said, "that we will require the use of the sitting-room at seven o'clock this evening. We may remain late and it is important that we should not be disturbed. For this reason I would ask you to have all of the members of your family retire early. When we are through and it is time for us to leave I will call you so that you may let us out. Do you understand?"

"Perfectly," she replied, with downcast eyes. "I will see that everything is prepared, and after that shall retire and wait until thee summons me."

On the night in question she carried out all of the orders with literal exactness. But she could not rest. The words of the British officer had filled her with curiosity and uneasiness. What did it mean? What was the object of this mysterious conference? Finally she could remain in her room no longer. She crept silently downstairs in her stockinged feet and took up a position outside of the door where the officers were assembled. By pressing her ear close to the crevices of the panels she could hear the talk from within. The words "Washington" and "Whitemarsh" attracted her attention and presently she obtained a connected story of their plans.

She was shocked, and with reason. What she had heard was an order for all the British troops to march out on the evening of the fourth to attack the army of General Washington, then encamped at Whitemarsh. She knew what that would mean only too well. Taken unawares by superior numbers, the patriot army would be destroyed. And that destruction meant that the torch of liberty would be extinguished—the hope of freedom would be destroyed.

Lydia Darrah crept silently upstairs again and went to bed, but not to sleep. She was depressed and disheartened. The thought that the lives of Americans might be lost in vain was intolerable. And while the members of her family slept soundly, and the officers in the room below perfected their plans, she wondered what could be done to avert the threatened calamity.

While her mind was filled with conflicting thoughts there came a rap at her door and the voice of the Adjutant-General saying that they were ready to leave. She remained perfectly quiet and then he knocked a second time and louder than before. Still no answer and this time he pounded with his fists. She arose, and taking her time to dress, appeared at the door, candle in hand, and pretended to be very drowsy. He apologized for having aroused her from sleep and left the house with his companions.

From that moment she was so agitated that she could neither sleep nor eat. The question was how to get the information to General Washington. She dare not confide in any one—not even her husband. She decided to go to Whitemarsh herself. In order to furnish a plausible excuse she informed the members of her family that it was necessary to get a sack of flour from the mill at Frankford. Her husband protested.

"Send one of the servants," he said. "There is no good reason why thee should make such a long trip."

"No," she replied resolutely. "I shall go myself."

"But at least," he pleaded, "take one of the servant maids with thee."

"I shall go alone," she insisted with a determination that surprised and conquered him.

William Darrah learned on that occasion that a Quakeress,

though placid in appearance, can be quite as obstinate as other members of her sex. He gazed wonderingly at the poke-bonneted woman as she left the house and started in the direction of General Howe's headquarters in order to get the requisite pass to get through the British lines.

General Howe received her kindly, if not almost jovially. He knew that the Adjutant-General of his army was quartered at the Darrah home, and he looked on Lydia as an interesting but harmless rebel. He was surrounded by members of his staff and they, like their superior, were disposed to jest with the Quakeress. But finally the coveted pasteboard was handed to her.

"Don't stay long," he smiled. "Your British guests will miss you."

The moment she received the pass she hurried away and once out of sight of the general's headquarters she almost ran until she reached Frankford. She left her bag at the mill, and saying she would return for it in a little while, continued her journey to Whitemarsh.

Washington had camped at this place after resting for a few days at Perkiomen Creek. He was reënforced by 1200 Rhode Island troops from Peekskill, under General Varnum, and nearly 1000 Virginia, Maryland and Pennsylvania soldiers. He was now within fourteen miles of Philadelphia. By a resolution of Congress all persons taken within thirty miles of any place occupied by the British troops, in the act of conveying supplies to them, were subjected to martial law. Acting under the resolution, Washington detached large bodies of militia to scour the roads above the city, and between the Schuylkill and Chester, to intercept all supplies going to the enemy.

This served a double purpose. It harassed Howe by preventing him from receiving the supplies and gave them to the Continentals. All this time Washington was observing a prudent policy. He was anxious to fight, but he was only willing to do so under circumstances that would be advantageous to himself. He had many critics of this policy, and some of them said nasty things, but Washington held steadily to his purpose in spite of good and evil reports.

Lydia Darrah plodded along to Whitemarsh, oblivious alike of the inclemency of the weather and her personal discomfort. Her one thought was to get the warning to Washington, for whom she had a respect and reverence that bordered on veneration. After leaving the mill at Frankford she encountered but few persons, and these looked upon the little Quakeress with only a listless curiosity.

It was when she had almost reached her destination that she began to feel footsore and weary. She was filled with a great desire to sit by the roadside and rest, but she resisted the natural inclination and kept on to the end. Within that frail body and beneath those modest and peaceful garments there was a grim determination that was Spartan-like in its persistence and its ignoring of pain and suffering.

Just before she reached her goal she saw a mounted Continental officer. His back was turned to her and she debated the advisability of speaking to him. Before she reached a conclusion he had twisted about in his saddle and looked in her direction. The recognition was mutual. He was a young American officer of her acquaintance, Lieutenant Colonel Craig of the light horse. He was evidently amazed at seeing her in such a place, and, riding over, touched his hat.

"Have you lost your way?" he asked, and before she could answer he added, "and how did you get through the British lines?"

She smiled sweetly in spite of her fatigue.

"I came to get flour at the mill in Frankford. General Howe was good enough to give me a pass."

"But you are beyond Frankford," he protested.

"Perhaps," she said hesitatingly, "I may be in search of my son who is an officer in the American army."

"Perhaps," retorted Lieutenant Colonel Craig, doubtfully.

By this time several soldiers on foot came in the direction of the speakers. Lydia became nervous and ill at ease. She plucked at his coat.

"Dismount and walk aside with me," she whispered. "I have something to tell you."

He complied with her request, wonderingly. The Lieutenant Colonel and his companions constituted a squad that had been sent out by Washington to watch the roads and to gather information concerning the enemy. Little did he suspect that such important news was at hand. They walked some yards from the soldiers.

"Now," he commanded, "tell me what in the world you are doing so far from home."

"Lieutenant," she cried in a voice that trembled in spite of herself, "I came to warn General Washington that General Howe intends to attack the Continental army. He hopes to find General Washington unprepared."

"How do you know this?"

"I overheard it last night. The Adjutant-General and other officers met at my house to make their plans. I felt that General Washington must be warned and I walked here for that purpose."

The eyes of the young officer almost stared out of their sockets. He gazed down at the frail woman in amazement and admiration.

"Shall I take you to the General?"

"No, it is sufficient for you to know. It shall be your duty to tell him. And you must agree not to reveal your source of information. If it was known that I came here it would go hard with me—it might mean my death."

"I promise!" he said, solemnly.

Then and there the Quakeress told him all that had taken place in her house at the conference among the British officers. She had an excellent memory and was able to give him all the details of the proposed attack. As she concluded she said:

"You must not reveal my identity—even to your men."

"It shall be as you wish, and now you must rest and have food."

She protested feebly, but he was not to be gainsaid, and insisted upon escorting her to a nearby farmhouse where she might obtain food and also rest for a while before taking the long walk back to the city. She urged him to go to Washington at once, saying the message he had to convey was more important than her personal comfort. But he was a gentleman as well as a patriot and he did not leave her until she had been safely housed and her wants attended to. On leaving he stooped and kissed her hand.

"You have saved the army," he said, "and you will not be forgotten as long as liberty endures."

She did not stay long, and, after a light meal, left for the return to Philadelphia. She paused at Frankford to get the sack of flour, which she carried with her as a proof of the statement that she had gone to the mill. Fortunately she reached her home safely, and apparently the incident after that was forgotten by the other members of the household.

But she was in a state of high nervous tension until she could be assured of the safety of the Continental army. She waited eagerly for the departure of the British. It was about forty-eight hours after her return from Whitemarsh that the beating of drums and the marching of many feet announced the departure of the troops for the purpose of surprising Washington. Lydia Darrah stood on the sidewalk as the glittering cavalcades passed by, apparently a non-important unit in the mass of spectators, but actually the heroine, if not the most important figure, of the drama that was to be enacted. After the last of the soldiers had departed she retired to her room in a fever of apprehension that was not to be allayed until she had received definite news of the encounter between the two armies.

General Howe was in high good spirits. He felt that he was going to catch the "old fox" sleeping, and the thought made him chuckle with delight. The town was full of Tories, too, and many of them would not have been displeased if the "rebels" received a crushing blow. But Lydia Darrah, in her darkened chamber, hoped and prayed that all might go well with Washington and his men.

In the meantime, at Whitemarsh, preparations for meeting the enemy were going on in the Continental army. Washington was impressed with the information brought to him by Lieutenant Colonel Craig. On the day of the 4th the Commander-in-chief received word from Captain Allen McLane, a vigilant officer, which confirmed the warning carried to the camp by Lydia Darrah. He made his dispositions to receive the meditated assault, and in the meantime sent McLane, with 100 men, to reconnoiter. This gallant officer met the van of the enemy at eleven o'clock at night on the Germantown road, attacked it and forced it to change its line of march.

But it was three o'clock in the morning before the alarm gun announced the approach of the main body of the British army. They appeared at daybreak and took their position at Chestnut Hill within three miles of Washington's right wing. Here the invaders met with a second surprise. Far from being unprepared, a detachment of the Pennsylvania State Militia sallied forth and gave battle to the redcoats. It was a draw, with a few dead and wounded on each side, and the British general in charge exclaimed:

"They don't seem to be a bit surprised!"

General Howe passed the day in reconnoitering and at night changed his ground and moved to a hill on the left within a mile of the American line. He wanted to get into action, but Washington, with great military shrewdness, declined to accommodate him. There were several sharp skirmishes at Edge Hill, and other points thereabouts, in which Morgan's Riflemen and the Maryland Militia were concerned, but no general engagement.

On the morning of the seventh there was every evidence that Howe meditated an attack on the left wing. This was what Washington most desired and his hopes ran high as he prepared for a warm and decisive action. In the course of the day he rode through every brigade explaining how the attack was to be met and exhorting the men to remember that they were fighting in the cause of liberty. He urged them to depend mainly upon the bayonet and to be on the aggressive always. Both his words and his manner impressed them, but especially his manner, for Washington had a demeanor at once grave and determined, which filled his followers with confidence.

The day wore on to its close with nothing but minor skirmishes. The reports show that Morgan's Riflemen and the Maryland Militia under Colonel Gist did brave work in this regard. An attack was next expected during the night, but it never occurred. The spirit displayed by the Americans, and especially their preparedness, had a discouraging effect upon the invaders.

When the first gray tints of dawn appeared it was seen that the British army was in motion again. But they did not advance toward the Americans. On the contrary they filed off to the right where long strings of fires were lit; behind these fires the redcoats silently departed in the direction of Philadelphia.

They had come on a fool's errand—like the king's soldiers in the couplet, they had marched up the hill and then marched down again.

Washington immediately detached light firing parties to fall upon the rear of the departing army, but they had secured too good a start to be very seriously damaged. The Continentals did, however, succeed in worrying the redcoats and in making them regret they had left Philadelphia.

Washington was sorry that there had not been a battle, and writing to the President of Congress at the time said:

> "I sincerely wish they had made an attack; as the issue in all probability, from the disposition of our troops and the strong situation of our camp, must have been fortunate and happy. At the same time *I* must add, that reason,

> prudence and every principle of policy forbade us from quitting our post to attack them. Nothing but success would have justified the measure; and this could not have been expected from their position."

It was a sorry procession of Englishmen that filed through the streets of Philadelphia after this historic retreat—because it can only be called a retreat. They had gone out with high hopes; they had returned—figuratively speaking—with their tails between their legs. They had expected to throw themselves upon a camp of sleeping and unprepared men; they had encountered a spirited and fully prepared foe. The Tory ladies who lined the sidewalks of the city felt sorry for the non-conquering heroes. But one woman watched that mournful march with pleasure, the woman who was chiefly responsible for it—Lydia Darrah.

On the night after the return of the British troops the Adjutant-General of the army sent for Lydia Darrah. He requested her to come to his room as he wished to put to her some important questions. She followed, quaking in her shoes. She felt that some one had betrayed her, and prepared to suffer the consequences.

"What I wish to know," he said, after she had been seated, "is whether any of your family was up after eight o'clock on the night that I conferred with the other officers in your sitting-room."

She shook her poke-bonneted head.

"Thee knows that we all went to bed at eight o'clock," she answered.

"I know that *you* were asleep," he said with emphasis, "because I had to knock at your chamber door three times before you were aroused. But I wondered if any one else was about."

"Why?"

"Because some one must have given Washington information concerning our march. I know you were in bed; you say the others were also. I can't imagine who gave us away unless the walls had ears. When we reached Whitemarsh we found all their cannon mounted and the soldiers ready to receive us. Consequently, after wasting days in marching and counter-marching, we were compelled to come back here like a pack of fools."

"I sympathize with thee," she said, but if one could have peeped beneath the folds of that poke bonnet one would have sworn there was a twinkle in those demure eyes and a smile of satisfaction upon that placid face.

And who will have the heart to find fault with the brave Quakeress for the twinkle, the smile and the white lie?

A Chapter from
The World's Greatest Military Spies and Secret Service Agents, 1917
By George Barton

MISS EDITH CAVELL

FIRST MARTYR OF THE GREAT WAR

WHEN Baron von der Lancken permitted the execution of Miss Edith Cavell, he furnished the first martyr of the Great World War. He did more than that. He dealt Germany a blow that robbed it of the respect of civilization. There had been many unpardonable and detestable acts before that event, but when this gentle Englishwoman was placed before a firing squad, the shot that took her life was heard around the world, and decent men and women, regardless of race or religion, instinctively arrayed themselves against the Kaiser and his brutal system. It was the death knell of tyranny, and in her own way this little woman did as much for the cause of liberty as a division of infantry or a squadron of battle-ships.

She was a teacher and a nurse, and before the war was a directress of a home for nurses in Brussels. Her whole life had been spent in doing good for others, and there is every reason for believing that the alleged acts for which she was executed were prompted by a love of humanity. In the beginning there was no suggestion that she had been guilty of espionage, but when the wrath of the world was aroused over her death, her stupid and cruel executioners began to speak of her as " the spy Cavell." The German Chief of the Political Department in Belgium was warned that the death of Miss Cavell would disgust the world, but he laughed cynically and said, "I am sure the effect will be excellent." It was excellent because, by laying her life on the altar of liberty, this courageous and lion-hearted woman helped to redeem the world.

It was shortly after her arrest, on August 5, 1915, that the matter first came to the attention of Brand Whitlock, the United States Minister to Belgium. It was reported that she had been taken into custody on the charge of aiding stragglers from the Allied armies to cross the Belgian frontier into Holland. It was alleged that she gave them money, clothing and information concerning the route to be followed. At that time the affairs of Great Britain in Belgium were being cared for by the American Minister. A cable-gram of inquiry from London caused Mr. Whitlock to write to the German authorities to ask if it were true that Miss Cavell had been arrested, and if it were true, that authorization be given to Gaston de La Leval, the legal counselor of the American Legation, to take up the matter of her defense. There was no answer to this communication, and a day or so later Mr. Whitlock wrote a similar letter to Baron von der Lancken, Chief of the Political Department. This brought a response. The Baron admitted that Miss Cavell had been arrested, and he added:

"She has herself admitted that she concealed in her house French and English soldiers, as well as Belgians of military age, all desirous of proceeding to the front. She has also admitted having furnished these soldiers with the money necessary for the journey to France, and having facilitated their departure from Belgium by providing them with guides, who enabled them to cross the Dutch frontier secretly. Miss Cavell's defense is in the hands of the advocate Braun, who, I may add, is already in touch with the competent German authorities.

"In view of the fact that the Department of the Governor-General, as a matter of principle, does not allow accused persons to have any interviews whatever, I much regret my inability to procure for M. de Leva! permission to visit Miss Cavell, as long as she is in solitary confinement."

This was disappointing, but it did not dampen the ardor of the American officials. Mr. Hugh Gibson, the Secretary of the Legation, had a premonition that Miss Cavell was doomed to death even before she was tried, and this filled him with an intense desire to do everything in his power to avert the tragedy. In this he was seconded ably by Monsieur Leval, who, although a Belgian, and thus in the black books of the Germans, did not spare himself any effort in a brave attempt to save the unfortunate woman.

Monsieur Leval wrote to the lawyer Braun, who said that he had found it impossible to attend to the case and that he had turned it over to his friend and associate, Mr. Kirschen. Thereupon the Belgian got into communication with Kirschen, and explained to him the deep interest that was felt in the case by the American Legation. One of the difficulties of the situation lay in the fact that lawyers defending prisoners before the German Military Court were not allowed to see their clients before the trial, and were not permitted to know what was in possession of the prosecution. It was playing the game with loaded dice, but that was the German way all through the war. When all of these things had been explained to Monsieur Leval he said that the least he could do would be to attend the trial to see that Miss Cavell was given a semblance of her rights.

"But, my dear sir," protested the advocate, in great alarm, "that will never do. You must not think of such a thing. Your presence would do Miss Cavell more harm than good. The Judge would resent the attendance of the representative of the American Legation. If you really desire to help the prisoner, you will stay away."

Astonishing as this may seem, it was the truth. Consultation with those who were familiar with the situation proved that Mr. Kirschner was correct, and so, with a heavy heart. Monsieur Leval remained away from the sittings of the Court. The trial began October 7, and ended the next day. Miss Cavell was tried under paragraph 58 of the German Military Code, which says:

"Any person who, with the intention of aiding the hostile Power or causing harm to German or Allied troops, is guilty of one of the crimes of paragraph 90 of the German Penal Code, will be sentenced to death for treason."

The paragraph 90 thus referred to is that of "conducting soldiers to the enemy." All of the legal authorities who have gone into this phase of the case agree that it was a strained interpretation of the facts to try Miss Cavell under this section of the law. Her perfect candor, which would have helped her in any civilized court, only helped to seal her fate with her barbarous judges. She admitted that she had helped soldiers to cross the frontier, and that some of them had written to her from England thanking her for what she had done. She was fearless enough to say that she had helped them to escape because she thought they would be shot by the Germans if they did not get out of Belgium. After all the evidence was in—and it was all one-sided—the Public Prosecutor asked the Court to pass sentence of death on Miss Cavell and eight other prisoners.

Monsieur Leval then asked permission to see Miss Cavell, and also asked that Mr. Gahan, the English Chaplain, be permitted to visit her. He received a flat refusal. They told him he could not see her until the judgment was pronounced and signed. It was also decided that Mr. Gahan could not visit her, but that she could see any of the three German Protestant clergymen attached to the prison.

While her friends on the outside were trying to save Miss Cavell, she was awaiting her fate with Christian fortitude. One of her fellow prisoners was Dr. Hostelet, of Brussels. He escaped with a five years' sentence, and when the armistice was signed, was released. Like all who came in contact with the heroic English woman, he was filled with admiration for her calm courage. He had known her before her arrest, and was familiar with the whole circumstances surrounding the case. Writing of those earlier days in Brussels, he says:

"In my frequent visits to Miss Cavell, I was able to see the risks she was running. The presence of a lot of men was obvious as soon as one entered the house—voices, songs, cries. I often pointed this out to her, and she replied calmly and resignedly:

'What would you? I cannot impose silence on them.' She even consented to let them go into town to amuse themselves. I remember her fright when one night some of them came back singing and disorderly, scandalizing the neighborhood.

"It was then that I and some other friends determined to put these dangerous guests in private houses or with reliable innkeepers. But the more we housed, the more came. One day six guides arrived bringing thirty men concentrated at Mons and sent to Rue de la Culture (Miss Cavell's home). At this time the home became publicly known as a refuge for fugitive soldiers. I was very worried and went to try to induce her to break off all relations for a time with this group of guides and soldiers, telling her that the work itself was imperiled and must be diverted into other channels.

"We had sure knowledge, too, that some suspicious persons knew of our prearranged signals. But she would not listen. 'Nothing but physical impossibility, lack of space or lack of money, would make me close my house to Allied fugitives.' So she went on, never ceasing her devotion to the work until the German police got on her track and made three perquisitions in her house, after which she was arrested. In her trial she was accused of recruiting, but she only spoke the truth when she replied: 'My object was to get the men sent to me across the frontier; once there, they were free.' She was also accused of espionage. Denial here was absolutely justified. That espionage was facilitated through her is certain, but she never took an active part in it. Absorbed in her work as head of a nurses' school, she never dreamt of running a recruiting office or a spy service. She wished to save men, Englishmen first, then Allies, and she gave herself up entirely to this humanitarian and patriotic work."

Monsieur Leval made a full report to Brand Whitlock, the American Minister, describing what he had done to assist Miss Cavell during the trial. He tells of the request of the Public Prosecutor to the Court, asking that the death sentence be passed on Miss Cavell, and then adds:

"After I had found out these facts, I called at the Political Division of the German Government in Belgium and asked whether, now that the trial had taken place, permission would be granted to me to see Miss Cavell in jail as there certainly could no longer be any objection in refusing this permission.

"The German official, Mr. Conrad, said that he would make the necessary inquiry at the Court and let me know later on.

"I also asked that permission be granted to Mr. Gahan, the English clergyman, to see Miss Cavell.

"At the same time we prepared at the Legation, to be ready for every eventuality, a petition for pardon addressed to the Governor-General in Belgium, and a transmitting note addressed to Baron von der Lancken.

“On Monday, at eleven o'clock, I called up Mr. Conrad on the telephone from the Legation — as I had already done previously on several occasions when making inquiries about the case— asking what the military court had decided about Mr. Gahan and myself seeing Miss Cavell. He replied that Mr. Gahan could not see her, but that she could see any of the three German Protestant clergymen attached to the prison; and that I could not see her until judgment was pronounced and signed, but that this would probably only take place in a day or so. I asked the German official to inform the Legation immediately after the passing of said judgment so that I might see Miss Cavell at once, thinking, of course, that the Legation might take immediate steps for Miss Cavell's pardon if the judgment really was a sentence of death.

"Very surprised, to still receive no news from Mr. Kirschner, I then called at his house at 12.30, and was informed that he would not be there until about the end of the afternoon. I then called at 12.40 at the house of another lawyer interested in the case of a fellow prisoner, and found that he also was out. In the afternoon, however, the latter lawyer called at my house saying that in the morning he had heard from the Gentian

Kommandantur that judgment would be passed the following morning. He said he feared that the Court would be very severe with all the prisoners.

"Shortly after this the lawyer left me, and while I was preparing a note about the case at 8.00 p. m., I was privately and reliably informed that the judgment had been delivered at five o'clock in the afternoon; that Miss Cavell had been sentenced to death, and that she would be shot at two o'clock the next morning. I told my informant that I was extremely surprised at this because the Legation had received no information yet, neither from the German authorities nor from Mr. Kirschner, but that the matter was too serious to run the smallest chance and that, therefore, I would proceed immediately to the Legation to confer with Your Excellency, and take all possible steps to save Miss Cavell's life.

"According to Your Excellency's decision, Mr. Gibson and myself went with the Spanish Minister to see Baron von der Lancken, and the report of our interview and of our efforts to save Miss Cavell is given to you by Mr. Gibson."

The report of Hugh Gibson, the Secretary of the American Legation at Brussels, to Mr. Brand Whitlock, the American Minister, to which Monsieur Level refers, says, among other things:

"We sent a messenger to Baron von der Lancken, urging him to return at once to see us in regard to a matter of utmost urgency. A little after ten o'clock he arrived, followed shortly after by Count Harrach and Herr von Falkenhausen, members of his staff. The circumstances of the case were explained to him and your note presented, and he read it aloud in our presence. He expressed disbelief in the report that sentence had actually been passed and manifested some surprise that we should give credence to any report not emanating from official sources. He was quite insistent on knowing the exact source of our information, but this I did not feel at liberty to communicate to him. Baron von der Lancken stated that it was quite improbable that sentence had been pronounced; that even if so it would not be executed within so short a time, and that, in any event, it would be quite impossible to take any action before morning. It was, of course, pointed out to him that if the facts were as we believed them to be, action would be useless unless taken at once. We urged him to ascertain the facts immediately and this, after some hesitancy, he agreed to do. He telephoned to the Presiding Judge of the Court Martial and returned in a short time to say that the facts were as we had represented them and that it was intended to carry out the sentence before morning.

"We then presented as earnestly as possible your plea for delay; so far as I am able to judge, we neglected to present no phase of the matter which might have had any effect, emphasizing the horror of executing a woman, no matter what her offense, pointing out that the death sentence had heretofore been imposed only for capital cases of espionage and that Miss Cavell was not even accused by the German authorities of anything so serious.

"I further called attention to the failure to comply with Mr. Kirschner's promise to inform the Legation of the sentence. I urged that, inasmuch as the offenses charged against Miss Cavell were long since accomplished, and that as she had been for some weeks in prison, a delay in carrying out the sentence could entail no danger to the German cause. I even went so far as to point out the fearful effect of a summary execution of this sort upon the public opinion, both here and abroad, and although I had no authority for doing so, called attention to the possibility that it might bring about reprisals.

"The Spanish Minister forcibly supported all our representations and made an earnest plea for clemency.

“After some discussion Baron von der Lancken agreed to call the Military Governor on the telephone and learn whether he had already ratified the sentence, and whether there was any chance for clemency. He returned in about half an hour and stated that he had conferred personally with the Military Governor who said that he had acted in the case of Miss Cavell only after mature deliberation; that the circumstances in her case were of such a character that he considered the infliction of the death penalty imperative, and that in view of the circumstances of this case, he must de- cline to accept a plea for clemency, or any representation in regard to the matter.

"Baron von der Lancken then asked me to take back the note which I had presented to him. To this I demurred, pointing out that it was not a 'requete en grace,' but merely a note to him transmitting a communication to the Governor which was, in itself, to be considered as the 'requete en grace.' I pointed out that this was expressly stated in your note to him, and tried to prevail upon him to keep it; he was very insistent, however, and I finally reached the conclusion that, inasmuch as he had read it aloud to us and we knew that he was aware of its contents, there was nothing to be gained by refusing to accept the note, and accordingly took it back.

"Even after Baron von der Lancken's very positive and definite statement that there was no hope, and that, under the circumstances, 'even the Emperor himself could not intervene,' we continued to appeal to every sentiment to secure delay, and the Spanish Minister even led Baron von der Lancken aside in order to say very forcibly a number of things which he would have felt hesitancy in saying in the presence of the younger officers and of Mr. de Leval, a Belgian subject.

"His Excellency talked very earnestly with Baron von der Lancken for about a quarter of an hour. During this time Mr. de Leval and I presented to the younger officers every argument we could think. I reminded them of our untiring efiforts on behalf of German subjects at the outbreak of the war and during the siege of Antwerp. I pointed out that while our services had been rendered gladly and without any thought of future favors, they should certainly entitle you to some consideration for the only request of this sort you had made since the beginning of the war. Unfortunately our efforts were unavailing. We persevered until it was only too clear that there was no hope of securing any consideration for the case."

From another authority we have a description of what took place in the court room at the conclusion of the trial. It is from Dr. Hostelet who, as already explained, was a fellow-prisoner with Miss Cavell at the bar of German Military justice. Dr. Hostelet gives a vivid pen picture of that dramatic moment when sentence was pronounced against Miss Cavell and the others:

"The military prosecutor came in. With his high coloring, waxed mustache, elegant and brisk, he looked as cheerful as ever. He entered the reserved part of the hall, followed by the interpreter, the lieutenant, the prison commandant and the German chaplain. He took a large sheet of paper from the portfolio carried by his faithful attendant. Every one was silent, and instinctively we drew together. The prosecutor read the verdict in German as if he were reading a list of honors. Five times the sinister 'Todesstrafe' (death penalty) was heard. For Baucq, Miss Cavell, Severin, Mille. Thuliez and Comtesse de Belleville. I got off with five years.

"The interpreter signed to us to leave the room. I saw Miss Cavell leaning against the wall, cold and impassive. I went to her and said a few words of hope. ' Mademoiselle, make an appeal for mercy.' "It is useless," she answered placidly, "I am English and they want my life.' At that moment the sub-commandant of the prison came for her. With care and deference he led her out of the room; he seemed to have some grave and painful communication to make to her."

The night before her execution Miss Cavell wrote a number of letters, and it is significant that the thought of those she was leaving behind her was deeper than any consideration for her last hours on earth. One of these letters was directed to a young girl friend who was afflicted with an appetite for drugs.

Here is the remarkable communication, written on the very eve of Miss Cavell's tragic death:

"My dear girl:

How shall I write this last day? Standing where I stand now, the world looks already far away. I worried about you a great deal at first but I know God will do for you abundantly above all that I can ask or think, and He loves you so much better than I. I do earnestly beseech you to try to live as I would have had you live. Nothing matters when one comes to this last hour but a clear conscience before God, and life looks so wasted and full of wrong-doing, with things left undone.

"You have helped me often, my dear, and in ways you little dreamed of, and I remember our happy holidays with mother, and many small pleasures. I want you to go to England at once now and ask ... to put you where you can be cured. Don't mind how hard it is. Do it for my sake and then try and find something useful to do, something to make you forget yourself while making others happy.

"In God permits, I shall still watch over you and love you and wait for you on the other side. Be sure to get ready for this. I want you to know that I was neither afraid or unhappy, but quite ready to give my life for England.

"I am sending you my wrist watch by Mr. Gahan because it was always with me, and I know you will like to wear it. I will pray God for you at the last that He will keep you in His tender care. Forgive me if I have been severe some times ; it has been a great grief to remember it. I think I was too anxious about you this last year and that was why. I am sure you will forget it and only remember that I loved you and love you still.

"Edith Cavell."

Can any one read this communication without a thrill of admiration for the Englishwoman who not only met death courageously, but who thought of the welfare of others during her last moments on earth? We have no account of the execution beyond the fact that the heroic nurse was shot early the next morning. Monsieur de Leval makes a brief reference to it. He says: "This morning Mr. Gahan, the English clergyman, called to see me and told me that he had seen Miss Cavell in her cell yesterday night at ten o'clock; that he had given her the Holy Communion, and had found her admirably strong and calm. I asked Mr. Gahan whether she had made any remarks about anything concerning the legal side of her case, and whether the confession which she made before the trial in Court was, in his opinion, perfectly free and sincere. Mr. Gahan says that she told him she perfectly well knew what she had done, that according to the law, of course, she was guilty and had admitted her guilt, but that she was happy to die for her country."

Miss Cavell wrote another letter on the eve of her execution, and it was addressed to her nurses in the institution at Brussels. A framed copy of it in both French and English is to be found in the living-room of the Nurses' Home in New York city. It deserves to be preserved for posterity. The complete text of this eloquent and moving communication is as follows:

"Prison of St. Giles, Brussels.

"My Dear Nurses:

"I am writing to you in this sad hour to bid you farewell. You will remember that Sept. 17 brought to an end the eight years of my direction of the school. I was so happy to be called to help in the organization of the work that our committee had just founded. On Oct. i, 1907, there were but a few pupils. Now you are already quite numerous—fifty or sixty, I think.

"I have told you on different occasions the story of those early days and the difficulties that we encountered, even to the choice of words for your 'hours on duty' and 'off duty.' In Belgium all was new in the profession. Little by little one service after another was established, graduate nurses for private nursing, pupil nurses, the hospital of St. Giles. We supplied the institute of Dr. Depage, the sanatorium of Buysinghen, the clinic of Dr. Mayer. And now many are called upon—as you may be, perhaps, later—to nurse the brave wounded of the war. If this last year our work has decreased, it is due to the sad days through which we are passing. In happier days our work will renew its growth and its power for good.

"I speak to you of the past because it is wise occasionally to stop and look behind over the road that we have travelled and to note our errors and our progress. In your beautiful building you will have more patients and all that is needed for their comfort and yours. To my regret I was not always able to speak to you individually—you know I had much to occupy my time—but I hope you will not forget our evening talks. I told you that devotion to duty would bring you true happiness, and that the thought you had done your duty earnestly and cheerfully before God and your own conscience would be your greatest support in trying moments of life and in the face of death.

"Two or three of you will remember the little talks we had. Do not forget them. Having already traveled so far through life, I could perhaps see more clearly than you and show you the straight path.

"One word more—beware of uncharitable speech. In these eight years I have seen so much unhappiness which could have been avoided if a few words had not been whispered here and there, perhaps without evil intention, but which ruined the reputation, the happiness, the life even, of some one. My nurses should all reflect on that, and should cultivate among themselves loyalty and esprit de corps.

"If any of you has grievance against me I pray you to forgive me. I may sometimes have been too severe, but I was never willingly unjust, and I have loved you all, far more than you realize.

"My good wishes for the happiness of all my young girls, both those who have graduated and those who are still in the school, and I thank you for the courteous consideration you have always shown me.

"Your devoted Directress,

"EDITH CAVELL"

To death of Miss Cavell caused a wave of righteous indignation to sweep over the civilized world. At first the Germans pretended to ignore this sentiment which was undoubtedly doing great damage to their cause, but finally it reached a point where Dr. Alfred F. M. Zimmerman, German Under Secretary for Foreign Affairs, was moved to make a formal defense of the execution. Speaking to the staff correspondent of the *New York Time*s in Brussels, he said:

"It was a pity that Miss Cavell had to be executed, but it was necessary. She was judged justly. We hope it will not be necessary to have any more executions.

"I see from the English and American press that the shooting of an Englishwoman and the condemnation of several other women in Brussels for treason has caused a sensation, and capital against us is being made out of the fact. It is undoubtedly a terrible thing that a women has been executed; but consider what would happen to a State, particularly in war, if it left crimes aimed at the safety of its armies to go unpunished because committed by women. No criminal act code in the world—least of all the laws of war—makes such a distinction; and the feminine sex has but one preference, according to legal usages, namely, that women in a delicate condition may not be executed. Otherwise, men and women are equal before the law, and only the degree of guilt makes a difference in the sentence of the crime and its consequences.

"I have before me the court's verdict in the Cavell case, and can assure you that it was gone into with the utmost thoroughness, and was investigated and cleared up to the smallest details.

The result was so convincing and the circumstances were so clear, that no war court in the world could have given any other verdict, for it was not concerned with a single emotional deed of one person, but a well-thought-out plot, with many far-reaching ramifications, which for nine months succeeded in doing valuable service to our enemies to the great detriment of our armies. Countless Belgian, French, and English soldiers are again fighting in the ranks of the Allies who owe their escape to the activities of the band now found guilty, whose head was the Cavell woman. Only the utmost sternness could do away with such activities under the very nose of our authorities, and a Government which in such case does not resort to the sternest measures sins against its most elementary duties towards the safety of its own army.

"All those convicted were apparently aware of the nature of their acts. The court particularly weighed this point with care, letting off several of the accused because they were in doubt as to whether they knew that their actions were punishable. Those condemned knew what they were doing, for numerous public proclamations had pointed out the fact that aiding enemies' armies was punishable with death.

"I know that the acts of the condemned were not base ; that they acted from patriotism ; but in war one must be prepared to seal one's patriotism with blood whether one faces the enemy in battle or otherwise in the interest of one's cause does deeds which justly bring after them the death penalty. Among our Russian prisoners are several young girls who fought against us in soldiers' uniforms. Had one of these girls fallen no one would have accused us of barbarity against women. Why now, when another woman has met the death to which she knowingly exposed herself, as did her comrades in battle?

"There are moments in the life of nations where consideration for the existence of the individual is a crime against all. Such a moment was here. It was necessary once for all to put an end to the activity of our enemies, regardless of their motives;

therefore the death penalty was executed so as to frighten off all those who, counting on preferential treatment for their sex, take part in undertakings punishable by death. Were special consideration shown to women we should open the door wide to such activities on the part of women, who are often more clever in such matters than the cleverest male spy. The man who is in a position of responsibility must do that, but, unconcerned about the world's judgment, he must often follow the difficult path of duty.

"If, despite these considerations, it is now being discussed whether mercy shall be shown the rest of those convicted, and the life which they have forfeited under recognized law is given back to them, you can deduce from that how earnestly we are striving to bring our feelings of humanity in accord with the commandments of stern duty. If the others are pardoned it will be at the expense of the security of our armies, for it is to be feared that new attempts will be made to harm us when it is believed that offenders will go unpunished or suffer only a mild penalty. Only pity for the guilty can lead to such pardons; they will not be an admission that the suspended sentence was too stern.

"The weakness of our enemies' arguments is proved by the fact that they do not attempt to combat the justice of the sentence but try to influence public opinion against us by false reports of the execution. The official report before me shows that it was carried out according to the prescribed forms, and that death resulted instantly from the first volley, as certified by the physician present."

The official defense of the execution of Miss Cavell thus made leaves out several important features of the case. The complaint of the United States Government was not that Miss Cavell was a woman, but that those in charge of the trial refused to give the United States Minister to Belgium an opportunity to make a plea in her behalf. Even the ordinary courtesy accorded to the vilest criminal of being permitted, before dying, to have a clergyman of his or her own selection, was denied her until a few hours before her death.

Mr. James M. Beck, an eminent member of the Bar, and an authority upon international law, in denouncing the attitude of the German Government in this case, says: "Apart from the brutality of the whole incident there is one circumstance that makes it of peculiar interest to the American people and which gives to it the character of rank ingratitude. Our representative did advise the German officials that a little delay was asked by our Legation as a slight re- turn for the innumerable acts of kindness which our Legation had done for German soldiers and interned prisoners in the earlier days of the war before the German invasion had swept over the land. The charge of ingratitude may rest soundly upon far greater and broader grounds. . . .

"Under these circumstances it would be incredible, if the facts were not beyond dispute, that the request of the United States for a little delay was not only brutally refused, but that our Legation was deliberately misled and deceived until the death sentence had been inflicted."

After the war, the body of Miss Cavell was disinterred, and brought to England amid impressive ceremonies. The remains reached London on May 15, 1919, and there was a public funeral in Westminster Abbey, conducted by the Bishop of London and participated in by an enormous concourse of people. King George was represented by the Earl of Athlone, brother of Queen Mary, and among other distinguished persons present were the Dowager Queen Alexandra, Princess Victoria, Secretary of State and Mrs. Lansing and the American Ambassador and Mrs. Davis.

When the procession left the Abbey it passed through streets massed with people who stood with reverent attention while the coffin of plain oak was placed on the train for Norwich, the home of the martyred nurse. On its arrival at that place it was conveyed to the Norwich Cathedral on a gun carriage. After brief services conducted by the Bishop the interment took place in the local cemetery. The benediction was pronounced, the bugle sounded, and then the earth was thrown upon the coffin which contained the simple inscription:

EDITH CAVELL

Born December 4, 1865
Died October 12, 1915

A CHAPTER FROM
Celebrated Spies and Famous Mysteries of The Great War, 1919
By George Barton

DESPINA DAVIDOVITCH STORCH

THE MYSTERY OF THE TURKISH BEAUTY

WAS Despina Davidovitch Storch, the beautiful Turkish woman who led a curious existence in New York City, a spy of the Sultan, or was she the innocent victim of the espionage laws of the United States of America?

That is a question which will probably never be answered in a definite manner. Not that it is impossible to answer, but rather because there are so many interests involved and so many innocent persons concerned that a positive and explicit statement would fail to further the ends of justice.

For many months the representatives of the Department of Justice were on the trail of Madame Storch. They had reports concerning her movements from five great capitals, and the curious part of it lay in the fact that she appeared in each of these cities under a different name. In Paris, for instance, she was known as Madame Nezie; in Madrid and London as Madame Hesketh; in Rome as Madame Davidovitch; at the Biltmore, in New York, as Madame Despina, and at the Shoreham, in Washington, as the Baroness de Bellville.

Surely we have here the foundation of a mystery story of surpassing interest. When we add to the secrecy of her movements the further facts that she was born in Constantinople, that she was strikingly beautiful, that she was married to a Frenchman, Paul Storch, at the age of seventeen; that they were divorced and that he was fighting in the French Army at the moment she was suspected of aiding the enemies of France, it is not too much to say that we have here a real-life romance more absorbing than anything dared by the writer of fiction.

Madame Storch was in Spain at the time the war began in the company of a gentleman who shall be known simply as the Baron. She attracted attention there, as she did elsewhere, by reason of her uncommon beauty and her lavish expenditure of money. Officers of the Army and the Navy, and even the ambassadors of the countries at war were on her visiting list. They vied with one another in paying attention to this young woman—she was only twenty-three—who had the mere suggestion of a Turkish nose, but otherwise, as one man has put it, with features that complied with "Occidental standards of symmetry."

The Turkish beauty and the Baron were seen in the company of German agents while they were in Spain. The French police heard of this and as a consequence the couple hurriedly left Madrid. They remained in Havana for a time, and then journeyed to New York.

In that city a curious quartette was placed under suspicion by the Department of Justice. It consisted of Madame Storch, the Baron, a French count, and a little German woman, a middle-aged widow who had two children at school in this country. One ascertained by the secret police was that Madame Storch had no visible means of support, and that she always had an abundant supply of money, and always paid her bills promptly. Also—and this was considered important—her companion, the German woman, was known to have received $3000 from Count Bernstorff as "a loan."

It was a significant fact that the beautiful Turkish woman always stopped at the best hotels. Thus, according to the agents of the Department of Justice, she had registered at the Savoy in London, the Palace in Lisbon, the d'Alba in Madrid, and the Biltmore in New York. Few persons had a wider acquaintanceship, and we are told that British army officers attended the "little parties" in her suite at the Savoy in

London. Her special penchant, as one writer puts it, " was for diplomats and men in uniform—officers from many nations who constantly streamed through her quarters at the Biltmore in New York, and other hotels in whose ballrooms she was well known." The investigators in this country learned that she had a safe deposit box in one of the banks in New York, and when this was seized it was found to contain a great quantity of documents, including correspondence, plain and in code, that was said to have come from notable persons in all parts of the world.

Madame Storch seemed to lead a butterfly existence in this country. She was seen at many social affairs, and as she danced well and spoke French delightfully, she was not lacking in admirers. The fact that some of those who enjoyed her hospitality were connected with affairs of State gave her an additional importance. It was remarked that the Baron, who has already been mentioned, was a frequent caller. He usually came in the evening, and then there were long and serious talks. About this time she became aware of the fact that she was under official scrutiny. One day she had her trunks sent to a steamship bound for Panama, but a Government agent intercepted them and sent them back to the hotel. Truly the plot was thickening, but up to this time no actual charges had been made against Madame Storch. She was in the unpleasant position of being "under suspicion." Late in February, 1918, she obtained a French passport to go to Cuba by way of Key West. A companion obtained a passport at the same time. The Department of Justice was fully informed of all her movements, but there was no disposition to take any action until more was known of the woman and her associates and activities. But it was decided that she should not be permitted to leave this country—or, at least, not to get beyond the control of the authorities. She went to Washington and remained there for two days, and all the time the investigator was at her heels. After that she went to Key West, and at this point she was taken into custody. She was brought to New York and quartered in a hotel there with a companion pending a decision from Washington.

An official of the Department of Justice said at the time that Madame Storch had been living in New York at the rate of $1000 a month. She gave various explanations of her income, but none of them were satisfactory to the authorities. While in this country she received one payment of $3000 from an official of a foreign government. From the same source she had received three $1000 remittances, which she said were advances or loans from friends. The baron in the case was the son of parents whose loyalty to France was unquestioned. They were naturally disturbed at the notoriety achieved by their son, and insisted that he was in no way involved in anything that might have the shadow of disloyalty. Any suspicion which might have been aroused came from his devotion to Madame Storch. The United States Government accepted this explanation. The count concerned was a friend of the young clerk who, as the Marquis di Castillo, passed as a chum of King Alfonzo, of Spain, and on the strength of this connection tried to borrow $50,000,000 from J. P. Morgan & Co.

The German woman who completed the quartette first told the investigators that she made one hundred dollars a week as a dressmaker, but as she could not produce a list of her customers, her explanation was not accepted by the Government. She finally admitted that she had been in correspondence with a young officer of the British Flying Corps. There does not seem to have been any doubt but that one or more of the quartette had been in communication with Americans as well as others in foreign countries, but no specific charges of this nature were made against them.

Finally it was decided that all four should be interned and then deported under the head of "undesirables." It was stated at the time that if they were sent to France they would be dealt with by the French authorities. Telegrams were sent to Washington, and it was announced that the case was so important that it would have the attention of A. Bruce Bielaski, Chief of the

Bureau of Investigation of the Department of Justice, and John Lord O'Brien, of the office of the Attorney General. An effort was made to induce Madame Storch to make a frank statement, but she parried all of the questions that were put to her by the authorities. But there was a feeling that she would weaken in the end and that there would be important revelations. In Government circles it was whispered that the secrets of the German spy ring might be disclosed at any moment. One anxious day followed another, and just when it was thought that the lips of the beautiful Turkish subject were to be opened there came a totally unexpected denouement.

Madame Storch died suddenly at daylight in her headquarters at Ellis Island where she was being held pending action that would have sent her to France, possibly to face a firing squad.

It was the dramatic close to a puzzling case. Madame Storch said more than once that she would never return to France, and the dark-eyed little woman who was called a "modern Cleopatra" was as good as her word. She was not the first suspect who had died when it was supposed important revelations were to be made. It was said at the time that death, apparently natural, yet stunning in its swiftness, seemed to be the fate of the mysterious ones who might have told the innermost secrets of the Kaiser's secret service system in America.

Curiously enough, the three persons who were associated with her. and who had also been taken into custody as "undesirable" subjects, were also taken ill at the same time. They did not die, but when the breath left the body of Madame Storch, the officials of the United States Government gave up all hope of learning the truth concerning her mission in this country Her funeral was delayed, and the body lay in the morgue at Ellis Island for some days in the hope that some additional facts might be ascertained, but all to no avail.

Officials of the Government frankly admitted that death was from natural causes. They said there was no ground whatever for the suspicion of suicide—a suspicion that might have been natural under the circumstances. From the time of her arrest her physical condition gradually weakened under the emotional strain that overcame her when she realized the seriousness of her predicament. Her coolness in parrying questions fell away, she became subjected, downcast and morbidly gloomy. This downheartedness obsessed her from the time she was trapped into confession that she was at one time known as Madame Hesketh and was on intimate terms with the German secret service. She contracted a cold after a crying spell one night, and a few days after pneumonia set in. It was not a serious case, but in her despondency she probably welcomed death and made no effort to win back health and life.

The funeral of this strange woman took place in New York on April 1, 1918. The ceremony has been described vividly in the New York Sun of the following day. From that account the following extract is taken:

"An cxquisitely carved white coffin containing the body of Madame Despina Davidovitch Storch, the most romantic spy suspect America has yet known, was placed in a vault on the east slope of Mount Olivet Cemetery, Maspeth, Queens, yesterday afternoon.

Thus was drawn the curtain on a life which in twenty-three years knew more diplomatic intrigue than even the popular fiction spy heroine is given by Oppenheim and others.

"The burial was simpler than those of people who never reached the prominence of the Beautiful Turk.

Only one limousine rolled up to the vault after the hearse. It contained the grief -stricken Baron, his parents and a secret service man, who accompanied the French nobleman from Ellis Island.

"The five knelt on the soft earth about the grave, and James F. Fallon, the undertaker, said a short prayer. The Baron, whose infatuation for the Turkish spy suspect entangled him in the web of her intrigues, wept silently and cast a last look upon the vault as he was led back to the car.

"The funeral services were held behind locked doors. It had been requested that she be buried from the Greek Orthodox Church of the Annunciation, 310 West Fifty-fourth Street, but the pastor of that congregation refused to officiate unless it were proved the dead Turkish woman had at some time in her life been a worshiper in the Greek faith. The Baron could offer no such evidence, and so Undertaker Fallon secured the Reverend Robert R. White, pastor of the Faith Presbyterian Church of West Forty-eighth Street, to offer prayer in the funeral parlors, 14 East Thirty- ninth Street, before the body was removed to the cemetery.

"The Baron, accompanied by a secret service man, drove up to the Fallon place at noon, and met his aged parents there. They embraced and mother and son wept a little. The young Frenchman bore a plaque of roses and some lilies which he tenderly placed in the folded arms of the dead woman, and then knelt by the casket, praying, for two hours. His parents sat close by.

"He murmured over and over again, and some say the words were 'Forgive me,' and others, 'Cherie, Cherie' and like French words of endearment.

"A morbidly inquisitive crowd circled the doorway of the funeral church an hour before the scheduled time for the services. They lined the sidewalk six deep in front of the Hotel Touraine, opposite the Fallon place. They climbed on trucks and pushed around the hearse; many lined the windows of the lofty buildings across the street. None was allowed to enter the funeral parlors, which were guarded by a secret service man.

"A little after two o'clock the white casket, carried by two undertakers, came out of the building. The chatter of the crowd hushed, and all that stirred the quiet was the music of "The Girl I Left Behind Me" which echoed into the street, as the subway band, on an army truck, passed by."

Thus ended one of the most mysterious and romantic stories of the war. It is an unfinished story, and that fact only adds to its human interest. In considering the case it must be remembered that no criminal charge was brought against her. She was never even brought before a United States Commissioner, although the United States District Attorney was waiting to handle the case should the Washington authorities decide to try her in this country. In telling her story, so far as it is known, there has been an earnest effort not to do injustice to her memory, or to reflect upon those who were associated with her in her last days. For that reason, all names have been omitted. It is certain that the titled Frenchman, who adored her, was guiltless of any wrongdoing so far as his own country and the United States are concerned, and it is not the province of the writer to pass judgment on either Madame Storch or her associates. She died in her youth, far from the land of her birth, a mysterious "undesirable."

But what a plot might be woven from the facts that have been made known through the investigations of the secret police of the United States! The details cover all of the essentials of a story of love, romance, diplomacy and adventure. They are at the disposal of any budding novelist or ambitious dramatist who may have the desire to win fame and fortune with the pen.

A Chapter from
Celebrated Spies and Famous Mysteries of The Great War, 1919
By George Barton

MATA-HARI

THE ROMANTIC LIFE OF THE DUTCH-JAVANESE DANCER WHO WAS SHOT AS A SPY

FEW stones of the Great War contain more romance, adventure and tragedy than that of the Dutch-Javanese woman who was shot as a spy on the rifle range at Vincennes at the breaking of dawn on the morning of October 15, 1917.

Marguerite Gertrude Zelle, better known as Mile. Mata-Hari, lived in an atmosphere of mystery and mysticism. She was born in Java about 1877, the daughter of a Javanese mother and a wealthy Dutch planter. As a child she gave promise of the great beauty which came to her in later life. As a young girl she was tall and dark, with a wonderful skin that was almost bronze in color. She seems to have had natural talents of a high order, and was given opportunities for education not granted to the poorer inhabitants of that Dutch possession.

It is not strange that she should have had an unusually colorful life. One needs only try to picture her early surroundings to understand that her existence was to be an uncommon one in every respect. In the locality where she was born and reared there were many men of many races. Besides the Javanese there were Arabs, immigrant Malays, Chinese, Hindus and other Orientals and some Dutch and other Europeans. Among the educated Javanese there was a love of literature, and we are told that they were fond of romances, poems and chronicles of the olden days, and that many of them made translations from the Sanskrit and Arabic. Christianity did not thrive in the Islands, and the religions which predominated then, as now, were Mohammedanism, Brahmanism and Buddhism.

As a child, Mata-Hari roamed among the remarkable Hindu ruins which dotted Java; she visited the beautiful temples of Buddha, and peered over the edge of more than one terrifying volcano. Her father died when she was quite young, and her mother, in order to protect her from the dangers which beset a child in that country of mixed races, took her to Burma and placed her in a Buddhist temple to learn the art of dancing, and at the same time pledged her to the life of a vestal bayadere. It. was on this occasion that she was given the name of Mata-Hari. She must have remained there for nearly ten years, but when she was still in her teens she escaped from the temple. The escape occurred on the occasion of a great Buddhist festival where she met a young army officer. She fell in love with the man and the story has it that they were married, and that two children were the result of the union. One report says that the boy, who was the favourite of his mother, died suddenly, and that a post-mortem examination proved that he had been poisoned, and finally that the dancer, taking the law into her own hands, shot a discharged gardener, who was suspected of the crime. She fled from her home and going to Paris began the professional career which gave her a world-wide reputation. The husband, we are informed, died soon after this, and the other child, a daughter, is now supposed to be living in England.

Surely this may be regarded as a sufficiently interesting prelude to the sensational life of a woman whose life was to end before a firing squad on the plains of Vincennes. In Paris she created a stir when she appeared as an exponent of Eastern ritualistic dancing. That city which loves sensations, took the tall, handsome woman to its bosom. She became one of the fads of the day. She was almost instantly deluged with offers to appear elsewhere. Invitations came from London, Berlin, Vienna, and New York. It is interesting to note at this point that Mata-Hari became a special favourite in Berlin and Vienna.

She performed frequently before titled men of those two capitals. Among her dances were several sinuous ones that were performed with the aid of wriggling snakes. About this time the war began and she made her way to Spain, and afterwards to Holland. Later she went to England and finally found her way again to Paris.

But she found a different Paris from the city where she had made her first success as a dancer. The gay capital was in gloom. Amusements were tabooed for the time being, and even the gay Parisians thought of nothing but the war. The dancer did not enjoy this sort of thing. She was a child of pleasure, and for a time thought of leaving Paris for other parts. But something happened that caused her to remain there.

It was hinted that she was in correspondence with some of her former admirers in Berlin and Vienna. The finger of suspicion was pointed in her direction. Evidently she was unaware of this fact for she moved about freely and made no attempt to conceal her movements. She left Paris and went to one of the English towns where experiments were being made with the famous tanks which proved to be such an important factor in the war. On one occasion she was seen with a young English officer who had fallen under the spell of her charms.

It was currently reported that her arrest and conviction were due to a rejected sweetheart, the brother-in-law of a former French Minister of Finance and once a noted banker, but, however true that may be, it is certain that the first tangible evidence in the case came to light while she was in England. She did not remain in the English town, but made frequent trips to London, and it is presumed that the information she was able to gather about the tanks was transmitted from the capital. How she was able to communicate with the Germans was long a puzzle. During this period she visited by turns Holland and Spain, and it is not hard to believe that it was in these countries that she was able to obtain a trustworthy messenger to carry the English secrets to Berlin. In the intervals between these trips to the Continent she was seen walking along the Strand and the West End of London. It was difficult for such a person to remain unnoticed. Her reputation had preceded her, and she was described in the English press as a " high-class Indian Princess, who had been a priestess in India, and one who had acquired complete control of enormous snakes."

Indeed, her very prominence served as a cloak under which she was enabled to carry on her dangerous operations. Her repeated presence in the company of the young officer attached to the tank service eventually brought her under suspicion. The tanks, or armored motor tractors, were trump cards in the British war game, and that fact in itself caused the Government to watch over them with unremitting care. Presently came word that the Germans were working furiously on a special gas to combat the tank operations. This meant that in some way or other they had obtained information of what the British were doing in this connection. Where did the information come from? That was the natural question, and after some inquiries in the little town where the tractors were being manufactured, suspicion pointed to Mata-Hari.

For one thing it was discovered that she was always well supplied with money. After giving a famous "veil dance " she had practically ceased her professional work, so that it was evident that the cash was not coming from her public exhibitions. In the midst of the British investigation she suddenly left for Paris. Her arrival in the French capital was the beginning of the end for the famous dancer. The French Secret Police were on her trail from the moment she stepped on French soil. In Paris her name of Mata-Hari was translated to mean " Eye of the Morning." The Secret Service men smiled grimly at this as they followed her from the Cafe de Paris to Maxim's and finally to Armenonville in the Bois. They did not fail to take note of the fact that she was in the company of an English officer who wined and dined her, and seemed proud of the fact that he was permitted to be in her company. The young man wore in the lapel of his coat a little twisted brass dragon, the same being an official insignia denoting service with the tanks.

One of the American correspondents says that it was on June first, exactly a month before Generals Haig and Foch began their drive astride the Somme, that Mata-Hari returned to Paris. He adds: "And the first thing she did was to apply for a vise on her passports permitting her to go to Spain. San Sebastian was the place she mentioned, explaining that she wished to attend the horse races there. Her papers were stamped and sealed, and she left almost immediately for the fashionable winter resort in the south.

"Madrid, Spain, and Nauen, Germany, are in constant wireless communication. There were other radio stations, privately owned in Spain, which could flash messages to Germany, according to Allied officers, and, of course, there were innumerable German agents, spies and propaganda disseminators infesting the land of the Dons. Secret Service reports disclosed the fact that Mata-Hari was seen much at the San Sebastian race course in the company of a man who was looked upon with suspicion by the French Government. He was a frequent caller upon her at the hotel where she stopped, and it was reported that he made many of the big bets which she placed upon horses that did not materialize as winners. Soon Mata-Hari came back to Paris and to the apartment near the Bois Boulogne. And once more the limousine owned by the individual branded a Deputy began rolling up to her door twice a week and sometimes oftener."

The plot was thickening. About this time the French people began to get the first news from the Somme. They learned of the simultaneous Franco-British offensive. There the tanks went into action for the first time, and, according to General Haig's

report, his " land ships " scored satisfactory results. But at the same time there were some disquieting rumors. It was hinted that several of the tanks were put out of commission in a curious manner. The enemy seemed to be possessed of private information concerning the "land ships." A number of German officers were taken prisoners at the battle, and when they were pressed, admitted that they had received descriptions of the tanks weeks before, and that they had been given special training in the art of combating these new weapons of war.

Mata-Hari was still in Paris at this time, and it is likely that she read the news of the battle with more than ordinary interest. At all events, the cozy apartments which she occupied in the Bois de Boulogne proved to be a magnet for the French police. One evening an officer appeared there, and asked for Mata-Hari. She appeared, radiant in evening toilet. She greeted the caller with regal pride, her bronze-like skin slightly flushed and her head held high in the air.

"How may I serve you, sir? " she demanded.

The man was lost in astonishment at this tall, beautiful woman, but he managed to tell the purport of his errand in a few words.

"You are wanted at headquarters. Come with me."

For a fleeting instant her countenance lost its composure. Evidently she fully realized the meaning of the command. The game was ended and she had lost. Without another word she put on her hat and coat and followed the officer. From that moment she was a prisoner, and was watched day and night until her trial. The story of her trial has not been given to the world, and probably never will be. Indeed, one of the difficulties in telling the story of the spies of the Great War has been found in the reluctance of the authorities to tell any more than has been necessary. But it is not hard to picture this regal beauty facing her judges in the hall of justice. Much of the testimony against her must have been circumstantial, as it is in the case of most spies, but when the evidence had all been pieced together the jurist who presided over the inquiry was satisfied of her guilt. That, too, was the verdict of his associates, and one morning she was commanded to stand up and hear the verdict pronounced by the Judge. It came in the awful words:

"Guilty, and condemned to be shot for the crime of high treason!"

She went back to her prison cell to await the final summons, and it was in the gray dawn of a dull October morning that Mata-Hari heard her last hour had arrived, heard it with an impassive face and not the least sign of emotion. It was the fifteenth of the month, and when the dancer awakened in her cell in the prison of Saint Lazare she instantly realized that the preparations for her execution were going on.

Captain Bourchardon, the representative of the French Military Court that had condemned her to death, was there, so was the warden of the prison and her counsel, M. Clouet. The Protestant clergyman, who was to offer her spiritual consolation, paced the corridor, while two nuns, connected with the prison, entered her cell to assist her in dressing. Smilingly she thanked them while declining their friendly offices. Quickly, deftly, and with the air of one who is about to go on an ordinary journey she dressed, attiring herself in a dark dress, trimmed with fur, which she had worn at her trial. A felt hat and a long coat completed her outfit.

Nervously the little procession lined up and marched through the dark corridor of the prison. The men in the party were visibly affected. Mata-Hari, as has been said, "was mistress of herself and her emotions." There was a pause in the office of the warden. Here the condemned woman was given the opportunity of writing two letters, which she entrusted to her lawyer. Without further ado, she entered a military automobile, in the company of Captain Bourchardon and the two nuns.

Presently they came in sight of the fortress of Vincennes. If any emotions stirred Mata-Hari she did not betray them. Around about her were some of the most historic buildings in France. The castle which was used as a royal residence until the time of Louis XV, and which has since served the double purpose of a prison and a fortress, loomed up before her eyes.

She probably recalled that the structure had housed Conde,

Diderot, Mirabeau and other distinguished prisoners, and, if so, it made her hold her stately head a little higher. Nearby were the woods of Vincennes, where the people of Paris came for their outings. Absent now were the signs of merrymaking. War had changed all of that, and for the moment a grim tragedy was being enacted within sight of the Parisian playgrounds.

Mata-Hari was the first to alight from the automobile, and with a graceful inclination she turned to help one of the nuns to alight. The two nuns accompanied her to the office of the Governor, and after the final official formalities had been concluded they started for the rifle range, this time being accompanied by a squadron of dragoons. During the brief ride from the prison, and in the short time before the execution, there seemed to arise a sort of understanding between the dancer and the nun who stood by her right side. The one a woman of the world, and the other a woman of God. Differing in faith, appearance and mode of thought, they were yet both women. The one pale and spiritual, and the other dark and almost bronzed with an air of haughty defiance. The calm, religious life of the little nun was reflected in the serenity of her countenance. The pride of the tall, beautiful dancer was shown in the stoicism of her face and manner. If the unfortunate woman felt anything, it was the sympathy of the little nun, and in the clasp of the two hands there was a world of meaning.

The Paris correspondent of the New York Sun has given us a dramatic picture of those last moments. Let him tell the rest of the story:

"On the range all preparations for the execution were ready. A detachment of infantrymen in their blue-gray uniforms were drawn up, forming a hollow square—the targets being at the further end. The firing platoon of zouaves was in the center, the men standing at attention. The automobiles stopped at the entrance to the square and Mata-Hari stepped out.

She gazed unmoved, almost disdainfully, at the setting prepared for her final appearance, in much the same manner as she had regarded the audiences that had applauded the exotic dances with which she had startled Paris. In the background stood a group of officers from the Vincennes garrison, many of whom had been witnesses of the condemned woman's stage triumphs. With her lawyer on one side and one of the nuns on the other, she passed unshaken in front of the silent, waiting troops.

"Arriving in front of the targets, Mata-Hari bade these two good-by, embracing the nun as she stretched out her hands to a waiting gendarme who held the cord with which they were to be bound. As he fastened it about her right wrist the spy with the other waved a friendly little farewell to the second nun off in the background. When both were securely fastened she was left alone, standing erect, facing the muzzles of the twelve rifles of the firing squad. The commander of the platoon raised his sword and the volleys rang out, followed a second later by the report of a single shot—one of the squad had not pulled his trigger in unison with his fellows. Mata-Hari fell on her knees. A non-commissioned officer of the dragoons advanced and fired at close range. The dancer fell backward.

She had answered her last curtain call. The troops marched past the prostrate body and returned to their barracks to begin the day's garrison duties, while the corpse was taken to a military cemetery and buried in a section set apart for the interring of executed criminals."

Such is the dramatic and thrilling story, so far as it can be gathered from many conflicting sources, of one of the most notable women spies of the world's greatest war.

A CHAPTER FROM
Celebrated Spies and Famous Mysteries of The Great War, 1919
By George Barton

CHEVALIER D'EON

THE STRANGE
ADVENTURES AT THE RUSSIAN COURT

THE Chevalier D'Eon was not a military spy in the ordinary sense of the term, but his secret mission to the Russian Court, in the disguise of a woman, was the direct means of reëstablishing diplomatic relations between Russia and France and of preventing England from obtaining the services of 60,000 Russian soldiers to be used whenever the emergency might require them.

Charles Genevieve Louis Auguste Andre Timothee D'Eon de Beaumont was the full name of this curious character who took part in one of the most remarkable adventures in the history of war, politics or diplomacy.

Before he appeared on the scene Chancellor Bestuzhev of the Russian Ministry and the English and Austrian Ambassadors had been engaged in a long and perplexing negotiation which was expected to end in a new treaty between Russia and England. His English Majesty, King George II, was haunted by the fear that France and Prussia had designs on Hanover. To prevent this he wished to make an alliance against these countries with Russia and Austria. Empress Elizabeth of Russia did not display much interest in the proposition, but her Chancellor, Bestuzhev, was eager to consummate the plan because he had no love for the King of Prussia and believed that any extensions of that monarch's kingdom would be detrimental to Russia.

Bestuzhev's scheme was to raise 60,000 recruits who were to be placed at the service of England in return for a subsidy which was placed at five hundred thousand pounds. This was in January, 1755; but between the desire of the English cabinet to reduce the amount of the subsidy and the indifference of the Russian Empress, the affair dragged along for many months. Indeed, the patience of the English ambassador—Guy Dickens—was so sorely tried that he resigned in a huff and was succeeded by Sir Charles Hanbury Williams, one of the most notable men of the period, who determined to distinguish himself by bringing about the alliance which his predecessor at St. Petersburg had failed to accomplish.

Lord Holderness, the English Foreign Secretary, gave the new Ambassador to Russia minute directions concerning what he was expected to do at St. Petersburg. In a letter dated April 11, 1755, he said among other things: "On this occasion it will be proper to convince the Russians that they will remain only an Asiatic power if they sit still and give the King of Prussia an opportunity of putting into execution his ambitious, dangerous and long-concerted schemes of aggrandizement. His Majesty has authorized you, by your full powers and instructions, to do what may be necessary for preventing such a calamity."

The new Ambassador went to work with great energy and if the private letters and memoirs of the time are to be credited he soon found that he was engaged in a most expensive undertaking. Nearly everybody about the Russian Court wanted money and wanted it badly. Ten thousand pounds, it is stated, besides "the usual diplomatic presents" were given to the Chancellor. "An extraordinary gift" was made to the Vice Chancellor. After that the Secretary to the Cabinet had to be considered and a letter to London said that this person could be obtained "for fifteen hundred ducats ready money, and five hundred per annum pension." But the money grabbers did not end here, for the bribery continued all along the line.

As a climax to this wholesale palm greasing, a convention was signed on the 9th of August, 1755, the chief feature of which was that Russia's aid to England should extend to all the allies of King George and that on the first demand for help from England, Russia would march 30,000 men against Prussia. This arrangement was to be ratified two months from the date of signing, but in the meantime was not to be binding.

Such were the methods of diplomacy 160 years ago! Is it surprising that the word at that time should come to have a shady meaning?

But unexpectedly an obstacle arose. Louis XV of France wished to renew diplomatic intercourse with the Court of Elizabeth. The Empress was favorable to this but her ministers knew that if it were accomplished the new treaty with England would be "merely a scrap of paper"—that it would be consigned to the waste basket.

Every attempt on the part of the French authorities to communicate with her was frustrated. Presently a Frenchman, the Chevalier de Valcroissant, appeared in St. Petersburg. His mission was to ascertain the feelings of the Russian Court toward the French monarch. He found out sooner than he expected, and in a way he did not relish. Charged with being a spy, he was arrested and shut in the fortress of Schlosselburg. Louis XV was furious but helpless. France did not have the power to protest against this proceeding because Valcroissant was not an accredited agent; he had only been sent as a private emissary to get the lay of the land.

Louis XV was not the sort of a man to abandon an enterprise. He considered how he could penetrate the barrier of diplomats and spies who were surrounding the Empress Elizabeth. And suddenly he thought of the man to accomplish this seemingly impossible feat.

It was the Chevalier D'Eon.

This talented young man, who had written a pamphlet on the financial condition of France under Louis XIV, had gained the friendship of the king and was in the Secret Service of his country. He had distinguished himself as a soldier at an early age, and was noted for the success with which he had performed several confidential missions.

It was decided that he should go to Russia with the Chevalier Douglass, and that he should go in female attire. Douglass was to leave France quietly on the pretext of traveling for his health and his supposed woman companion was to be represented as his niece. Above all he was not to have any communication with any French officials whether in France or during the course of his travels.

His instructions were given in great detail. He was to enter Germany though Sweden, and to pass into Bohemia on the plea of examining its mines. On reaching St. Petersburg he was directed to make the acquaintance of any persons who might be able to help him in his enterprise. Among other things he had orders to ascertain the influence which was exerted over Elizabeth by her favorites and to send this information from time to time to Louis XV. No letters were to be posted in the ordinary way, but all negotiations were to be reported by means of a cipher code which was to be forwarded to private addresses in Paris.

The Chevalier D'Eon entered into the affair with much enthusiasm. His appearance easily lent itself to the disguise of a female. He was small and slight and had a pink and white complexion and his expression was gentle. A sweet voice helped to make his disguise complete. This exploit of the notorious adventurer afterwards gave him an unwelcome fame which he was never able to live down, although history proves that he was a brave soldier and had many manly qualifications. His defense for the remarkable escapade was love of country, a taste for adventure and the fact that a spy must do many things that would be distasteful to a soldier.

Before D'Eon left Paris he was given a copy of a French novel, which had concealed between the boards of its binding a letter from Louis XV to the Empress Elizabeth. It also contained a cipher which the Empress and her Vice Chancellor Woronzoff were to use in corresponding with the French king. It is a significant fact that this volume never left the possession of the young adventurer. He read it on all occasions—in his room at hotels and even while he waited for an audience with the officials of the Russian Court. Is it any wonder that he gained the reputation of being an omnivorous novel reader?

The little drama began when the Chevalier Douglass arrived at Anhalt and stopped at one of the hotels to await the arrival of his delightful niece. She arrived in due time, did Mademoiselle Lia de Beaumont, and made an immediate and favorable impression on all with whom she came in contact. Such charm! Such shyness! Such modesty and at the same time such sprightliness! Is it any wonder that Douglass and his young relative at once gained the attention of the best society of the place? They were pressed to make a long stay at Anhalt, but declined on the ground that it was necessary to proceed to the capital.

In St. Petersburg they stayed at the house of Monsieur Michael, the French banker, who was a man of eminence in the Russian city. One of the first persons to meet Douglass was the Austrian Ambassador. He was curious about the new arrivals.

"What are you doing in this country?" he asked.

The wily courier of the king was seized with a fit of coughing and at its conclusion replied:

"I am here by the advice of my physician, in order to get the benefit of a cold climate."

All the while the real purposes of Chevalier Douglass were in microscopic characters on the sheet of thin paper concealed in the false bottom of a tortoise shell snuff box. Every time he took a pinch of snuff he thought of his mission. Also he was sure that if he should be suspected and searched that the snuff box would escape attention and confiscation. But as the days went by the charming niece was seized with a desire to see the Empress, not in a public, but in a private audience.

How was this to be accomplished?

The French banker who was acting as host to the queer couple was acquainted with the Vice Chancellor, who had no love for the Chancellor. So he invited the first named personage to his house to meet Douglass and his "adorable niece." The Vice Chancellor was delighted with the newcomers and readily agreed to present the niece privately to the Empress.

The meeting took place in one of the large rooms of the palace and as soon as they were alone the fascinating young woman exclaimed:

"Your Majesty, I am not what I seem. I am the Chevalier D'Eon sent to you as the special messenger of Louis XV. It was necessary to come to you in this guise to outwit your court officers who were determined that no message from the King should reach you."

At first amazed, the Empress afterwards felt flattered that such extraordinary means should be employed to obtain her attention, and she made the supposed female sit down and tell her the story of how the ruse had been planned and executed. After that D'Eon told of the desire of the King to resume diplomatic relations with the Russian Court. Her Majesty was greatly flattered. The manner in which she had been approached appealed to her imagination, and she agreed that the deception of her ministers should be continued. In order that the scheme might be facilitated, she appointed D'Eon her reader, which not only gave him a reason for being about the Court, but also furnished him with ready access to her at all times.

In a very short time she gave him a written statement in which she expressed a willingness to receive and to accord "respectful treatment for any envoy of the King of France who would bring with him sufficient powers to sign a treaty." With this precious paper in his possession Douglass hastened to Paris to give it to the King. D'Eon, in the meantime, remained in St. Petersburg in order to see that there were no unexpected developments that would militate against King Louis XV. There can be no doubt but that it was the secret influence which Douglass and D'Eon had with the Empress which led her to neglect the treaty with England which the Chancellor had fully expected her to sign.

"I am sorry to say," writes the English Ambassador to Lord Holderness, "that it is impossible for the Chancellor to get her Majesty to put her signature to the treaty which we so much desire. He appears to be very much in awe of her." Little did the diplomats suspect that their carefully laid plans had been upset by the "charming niece" of the Chevalier Douglass.

In the meantime other events were occurring in other parts of the world which served to make still further impossible the thing which England had so ardently desired. King George had become alarmed over the unexpected delay and entered into a defensive alliance with the King of Prussia. By this the Prussian monarch agreed to defend Hanover. This treaty was signed at Westminster on January 16, 1756. The news was sent to the English Ambassador at St. Petersburg, who promptly communicated it to the Chancellor Bestuzhev.

That aged, if not venerable, diplomat swore violently. And little wonder, for it meant that his long-sought scheme to humiliate Frederick of Prussia and to gain England as an ally, had collapsed. After he had partially recovered his self-possession he exclaimed:

"This union between England and Prussia will be bitter news to her Imperial Majesty."

"Why so?" replied the innocent English Ambassador. "Such an alliance can offend no one but France."

In the meantime the treaty between England and Russia was still regarded as a desirable thing and Bestuzhev and the English Ambassador worked hard with that end in view.

The hint was given that some financial gifts promised by England had not arrived, but the English Ambassador assured the Russian Chancellor that it would all be received in due time and that if necessary the promised sums would be advanced at once. As a consequence of this there was much activity about the Russian Court. Finally the long deferred ratification took place on February 4, 1756, but there had been slyly added to the treaty a phrase stating that it would be valid only in case the King of Prussia attacked the dominions of his Majesty, the King of Great Britain. The English Ambassador strongly protested against this clause because it made his labor of many months and his splendid financial "gifts" practically useless, but he was obliged to accept the paper as it stood.

But the worst was still to come. When the Empress became fully informed of the treaty between Prussia and England she was furious, and immediately declared that the arrangement just made between her own country and England should be declared void. Bestuzhev was frantic at this order which destroyed the work which had cost him so much time and labor. Indeed, so far did he go that the Empress reprimanded him for his impertinence.

The changed condition of diplomatic relations in the world now made it more desirable than ever that France should be represented at the Russian Court. The Chevalier Douglass was sent by Louis XV to St. Petersburg for the second time. He reached there in April, 1756, and was so eager to present himself that late on the evening of his arrival he called on the Vice Chancellor and handed him a letter from the French King to the Russian Empress. The Vice Chancellor, who was in sympathy with the program of the French, made it a point to present the messenger from Paris to the Empress that very night. Elizabeth was not very well pleased that the Chevalier Douglass should be sent to her Court as an unofficial agent instead of an accredited minister, but in spite of this fact she received him graciously and listened to what he had to say. A few days later she sent for Douglass and gave him a note addressed to the French Minister of Foreign Affairs in which it was stated that it would be agreeable to her Imperial Majesty if the Chevalier Douglass was more fully authorized or accredited as chargé d'affaires, so that it would be possible for both sides to treat with greater authority on the matters included in his instructions. She added that this would not only be to the mutual advantage of both courts but would also tend to hasten their reunion in a diplomatic sense. It was further stated that notwithstanding the failure to make the Chevalier Douglass an accredited minister he would be treated with distinction and listened to with great consideration as being a person sent to Russia on the part of Louis XV.

Shortly before this meeting between the Empress and Douglass, the Chevalier D'Eon had returned to Paris, but during his stay in St. Petersburg he had won the friendship and favor of the Empress. He had on numerous occasions acted as her reader and his great knowledge of men and things in all parts of the world had furnished her with more than ordinary entertainment. She learned that he had a real knowledge of art and literature and also that while living in Paris he had been in the midst of many men distinguished in literature, politics and art. Also she had him recount to her his early experiences as the son of a Tonnere lawyer and the descendant of a good family. D'Eon was not the sort of a person to boast of his personal courage, but by close questioning she learned that he had been engaged in many military exploits which redounded to his credit.

As a result of all this she desired very much that the Chevaliers Douglass and D'Eon should be returned to her court as thoroughly accredited representatives of their Government, but while she was working to this end, her Chancellor and the English Ambassador were doing all in their power to prevent the consummation desired by the French king. Indeed, the English representative still had hopes of accomplishing the task he had been instructed to perform. His only fear seems to have been that the health of the Empress, which was not very good at that time, might become worse and leave the matter suspended, like Mohammed's coffin, between Heaven and earth. The Court was in what might be described as a state of uproar, and Sir Charles Williams, writing to Lord Holderness, says: "The state of the Empress's health has been extremely bad. On the 16th instant there was a ball at Court, and after the Imperial Ambassador of Austria was gone she told me she would dance a minuet with me. As soon as it was over she was so spent that she retired into her own apartments for a quarter of an hour. She then returned into the ballroom and taking me aside told me in a very affecting strain how ill she was. She said that her cough had lasted nine minutes and she could not get rid of it, and that she had quite lost her appetite. While she was telling me this she was seized with another fit of coughing that obliged her to retire, and she appeared no more."

In another letter addressed to his superior, Sir Charles says: "Last night the Empress was much worse. She intends if possible, however, going to Count Esterhasy's ball, which he gives in honor of the young grand duke next Wednesday, and there is actually a machine making to carry her Majesty from one floor to another without obliging her to mount the stairs. I leave your Lordship to imagine the alarm which this Court it in. I had much conversation last night with the Grand Chancellor on the present scene. He perhaps is less alarmed than other people, for the Grand Duchess is his friend and is governed by him. As her Imperial Highness is the person who in case of accidents will rule here, I think it will be well to inform the King of my observations upon her, which I can the better do because I often have conversations with her for long periods, as my rank places me at supper always next to Her Imperial Highness, and almost from the beginning of my being here she has treated me with confidence, and sent word by the Grand Chancellor that she would do so."

But all of the solicitude of the English Ambassador was lost. He could not get the Empress to agree to the reopening of negotiations looking to the treaty between the two countries. On the contrary she renewed her request to King Louis XV for an official representation of that country at the Russian Court. The Empress's request was given prompt consideration, for in July of the same year the Chevalier Douglass was accredited chargé d'affaires to the Russian Court, while D'Eon, the dashing young adventurer, joined him, no longer in woman's apparel but in the handsome dress of a fashionable young man. He was appointed and served with great success as Secretary of the French Legation at the Russian Court. It is very significant of the waning influence of the wily Chancellor in the esteem of the Empress, that he knew nothing of the arrangement by which Douglass and D'Eon were sent to St. Petersburg until these two persons had reached the frontier town of Riga.

This was an instance where French shrewdness got the better of English gold. Chancellor Bestuzhev was outwitted and outplayed at every stage of the diplomatic game. He realized, when it was too late, that he had been beaten by a French spy, disguised as a woman, and the recollection of it embittered the remainder of his life.

There was a dramatic sequel to this defeat, which fortunately for those concerned, did not have a fatal ending. Armed thugs entered the house where Douglass and D'Eon were sleeping and, rushing into the room, fired several shots at the young men.

They escaped with their lives and were content to regard the affair as an ordinary case of housebreaking. But if either of them had been called upon to point the finger of suspicion at any one, it would have been straight in the direction of Chancellor Bestuzhev.

A Chapter from
The World's Greatest Military Spies and Secret Service Agents, 1917
By George Barton

Printed in Great Britain
by Amazon

72752618R00045